KPF

Kohn Pedersen Fox

ROCKPORT

Kohn Pedersen Fox

GLOUCESTER MASSACHUSETTS

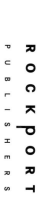

ROCKPORT PUBLISHERS

Editor: Aurora Cuito
Texts: Kohn Pedersen Fox
Graphic Design: Emma Termes Parera

Library of Congress Cataloging-in-Publication Data available

ISBN: 1-59253-043-5

10 9 8 7 6 5 4 3 2 1

Printed in China

For the past 26 years, Kohn Pedersen Fox has contributed to the built environment with a design philosophy firmly rooted in the belief that success is the result of collaboration and dialogue. The KPF creative process stresses an open exchange of ideas—both within the firm and more importantly, between the client and the firm—throughout the development of a project. Through this unique approach, "the comparative process," they are able to ensure that the client's needs and desires are addressed at each turning point in the life of a project. Ideas are not submitted solely for approval or rejection, but rather for discussion with the hopes of spurring additional solutions that will each help craft a more complete structure.

"The comparative process" is not restricted to its interaction with a client, however, a similar sentiment is central to the manner in which they weave their buildings into the environmental fabric. Each KPF building has its own personality, yet they all share an unending dedication toward creating a dialogue with their surroundings—a dialogue expressed by the shape and form of the buildings. The buildings aim to make an important contribution to the environment in which they are situated, but not to the point where they disturb the delicate equilibrium that exists in modern cities. KPF's buildings project a singular image but not at the expense of those structures that surround them.

Today's business climate makes it necessary for buildings to adapt to different roles and meet various internal needs, and many times this cannot be accomplished through the traditional edifice. KPF's buildings

stand apart from most commercial structures because of a unique style that they developed almost 20 years ago—an evolving style that remains fresh today. Buildings such as 333 Wacker Drive (Chicago), World Bank Headquarters (Washington, D.C.), Baruch College (New York), and DG Bank Headquarters (Frankfurt) exemplify their belief that the whole is greater than the sum of its parts. The buildings comprised unique, easily discernable parts that are smoothly integrated into one cohesive structure. By creating a building composed of individual parts that each addresses individual needs, KPF maximizes the given space and creates equilibrium between internal needs and external capabilities. Each empirical part of the structure contributes to the whole, just as the complete building augments the environment into which it is placed.

Creating buildings that meet the changing needs of their clients is paramount to everything they do yet they achieve this goal amidst an ongoing search for greater technical capacity and artistic enrichment. Their buildings exemplify the belief that the art of architecture and art of urbanism are inseparable, and that when a KPF structure is completed, the client has not only made a contribution to their future, but the future of a city as well.

IBM World Headquarters

Nestled within a landscape of 450 wooded, rocky acres some 50 miles from Manhattan, the IBM World Headquarters exemplifies KPF's demonstrated ability to respond to the natural context and produce an innovative work of architecture. The building offers IBM a strong and dynamic image, embodying the aspirations of a client with a tradition of progressive architectural patronage while it addresses a complex operational and programmatic brief.

Completed in 1997, the headquarters is the centerpiece of an existing corporate campus in this rugged, wooded setting that is surprisingly dramatic in character, with deep ravines slicing through the landscape. A relatively low-rise development was inevitable, adapting to the contours of the site to allow the 280,000-sq. ft. building to be comfortably accommodated.

The form of the new headquarters takes its cue from the world of architectural experiment, yet offers enormous practical advantages. Designed to interact with its natural surroundings as much as possible the building has a generous provision of controlled natural light and excellent views out to the landscape, and open terraces for relaxation and informal meetings. Effortlessly addressing the site contours, the building assumes an extended, tapering *Z*-shape which adapts well to the open space program required by IBM as a significant change to their corporate culture. The central wing includes areas of enclosed space for executive offices and meeting rooms. The connecting wings maintain a highly functional core-to-wall depth to accommodate the open office workstations. The internal, irregular spaces within the plan are utilized for conference rooms, services, and core functions.

The building is anchored to the ground by a base of natural stone, a contrast to the dominant aesthetic of stainless steel, aluminum and glass. The roof is considered as a "fifth elevation"—the conventional distinction between walls and roof is abolished. The careful attention to the use of materials and detail is seen equally in the two-story entrance lobby, where dark green granite is counterpoised by stainless steel and copper leaf, with a landmark "prow" bringing light into the heart of the building.

Location: Armonk, New York, US
Date of construction: 1995–1997
Client: IBM
Photographer: Peter Aaron/Esto
Gross area: 280,000 sq. ft.

Between the building and the lush vegetation of the woods, exterior gardens, which act as a transition space, were included in the project. They afford the users of the complex the necessary space in order to be able to delight in the views of the surrounding area.

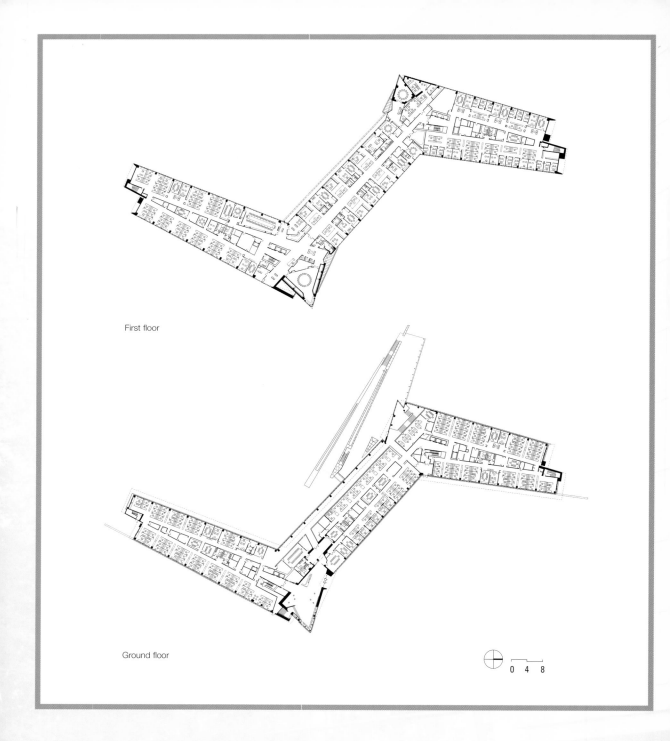

First floor

Ground floor

0 4 8

In the interior, the use of multiple angles to delimit partitions, false ceilings, the furniture, or the breaking up of the uniformity of the flooring, generate a great variety of perspectives that enrich the perception of the spaces.

The Province of South Holland sought an addition to the seat of the regional government, the Statenzaal, on the corner of The Hague's major park, the Malieveld. The commission was won through a European competition involving 25 competitors.

The site suggested a strategy of two building types: to the rear, a taller slab as a backdrop, and in the front, a lower *L*-shaped building attached to the existing Statenzaal. Together, the buildings create a courtyard. At the point where the two structures might have touched, they are held back, as if recoiling from each other. The resulting wide entrance welcomes pedestrians approaching from the city center.

The building design utilizes an innovative series of strategically placed social spaces which create a chimney effect to naturally ventilate the structure. The façade along the streets, strip windows set between horizontal bands of bricks, derives from the dynamic character of the building form and from the tradition of early 20th century Dutch architecture.

Location: The Hague, The Netherlands
Date of construction: 1998
Client: The Province of South Holland
Photographers: Christian Richters and E.G. Esch
Gross area: 258,000 sq. ft. (new building)
215,000 sq. ft. (renovation)

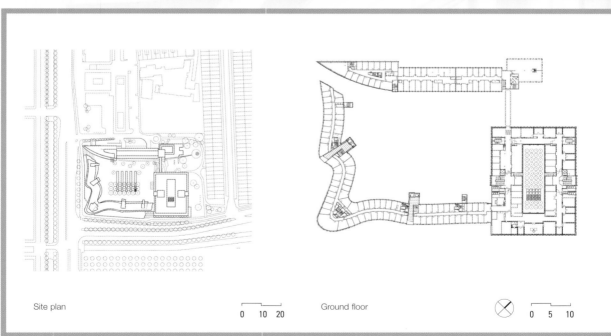

Site plan

0 10 20

Ground floor

0 5 10

Despite the generous dimensions of the building and the official character of the activities carried on there, they managed to achieve a cozy setting that feels near to the users. The forms and the materials used reduce the feeling of monumentality of the ensemble.

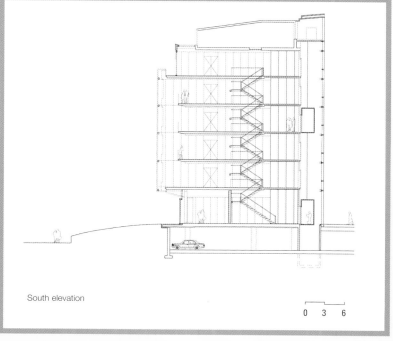

South elevation

0 3 6

This academic building for Baruch College occupies three quarters of a full block in lower Manhattan on Lexington Avenue between 24th and 25th Streets. Opposite the site is the University's recently completed Newman Library. Two blocks south on Lexington Avenue is the University's current academic facility.

The building is the center of Baruch's urban campus.

At the heart of the building is a great central room that steps towards the sun from north to south. This room is a vertical interpretation of the traditional college quadrangle.

The transformed quad connects three dominant pieces of the building: the business school, the liberal arts college, and the shared social amenities. The space functions as a central gathering space where students and faculty can meet and interact. The typical upper floors, linked by the common atrium, accommodate a variety of classrooms and offices. Large public assembly rooms and athletic facilities are located in the lower basement floors.

The massing of the building and the exterior wall systems address the zoning envelope and general context.

The building envelope maximizes the building floor plate relative to the sky exposure plane and eliminates excessive setbacks and roofs. Each elevation responds to internal program and exterior context with a range of cladding materials and window sizes. The five-story brick and stone base relates directly to the library across the street and to the scale of the neighborhood. The high-rise component is broken into parts. Layers of corrugated aluminum wall panel, ribbon windows, and curtain wall are detailed to define each elevation. Perimeter private offices typically have operable vents to regulate fresh air. Giant windows frame the central atrium on the north facade to provide a visual connection to the Newman Library and to bathe the public spaces in natural light.

Location: New York, New York, US
Date of construction: 1995–2001
Client: Baruch College
Photographer: Michael Moran
Gross area: 750,000 sq. ft.

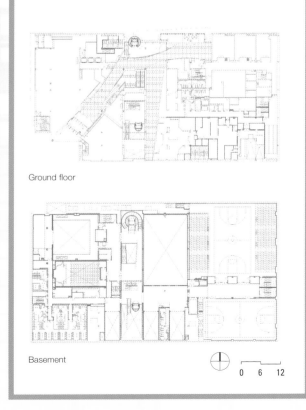

Ground floor

Basement

0   6   12

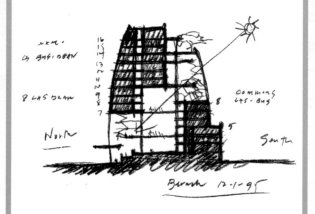

Sketches

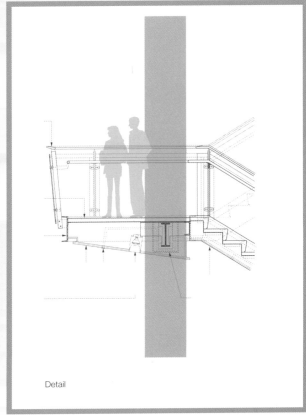

Detail

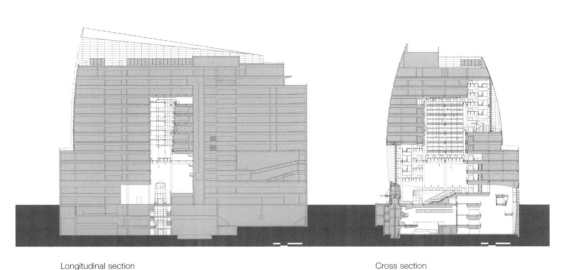

Longitudinal section

Cross section

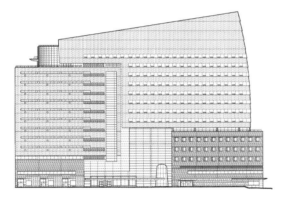

South elevation

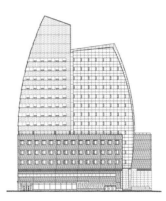

West elevation

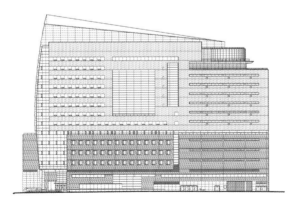

North elevation

0   3   6

The Gannett/USA TODAY Corporate Headquarters represents a thorough restudy of the office building. In its design, every aspect of the office environment was critically reconsidered, from the individual workstation, to the exterior form and cladding of the complex, to the ecology of the site. The resulting complex follows no familiar precedents. It is neither high-rise nor low-rise, provides consciously varied work settings, and looks unlike any other corporate headquarters. The client is a two-part corporate entity, comprising the headquarters of Gannett Co., Inc., a diversified news and information company, and USA TODAY, a national broadsheet.

The 700,000 sq. ft. building is situated at the intersection of two regional arteries, the Beltway and the Dulles Toll Road. It consists of two mid-rise structures for Gannett and USA TODAY, spiraling up from a base of shared facilities that wraps around an exterior "town square" at the main entrance. The northwest portion of the 30-acre site was judged most ideal for the U-shaped building, with the entry court facing southeast-capturing desirable sunshine while shielding it from the coldest winds, as well as highway noise.

Open in plan, the large floor plates easily support the primary functional requirement for newsrooms, production areas and corporate offices. The other half of the building is dedicated to auxiliary facilities and amenities such as a cafeteria, an auditorium, conference and training suites, a health club, a bank, a credit union, a concierge service, and on-site retail. The lobby is a high space connecting the two elevator towers, with a reception desk from which both elevator banks can be observed.

The glazed corridors running along the edges of the central courtyard make interior circulation visible, and foster a sense of community with the least interruption of the office floors. Pulling the elevators outside of the building volume and enclosing them in glass adds to the sense of activity as seen from both corridors and courtyard, while it reduces the obstruction of floor layouts that elevators typically entail.

Location: McLean, Virginia, US
Client: Gannett Co., USA TODAY, Hines
Date of construction: 1997–2001
Photographers: Timothy Hursley and KPF
Gross area: 700,000 sq. ft.

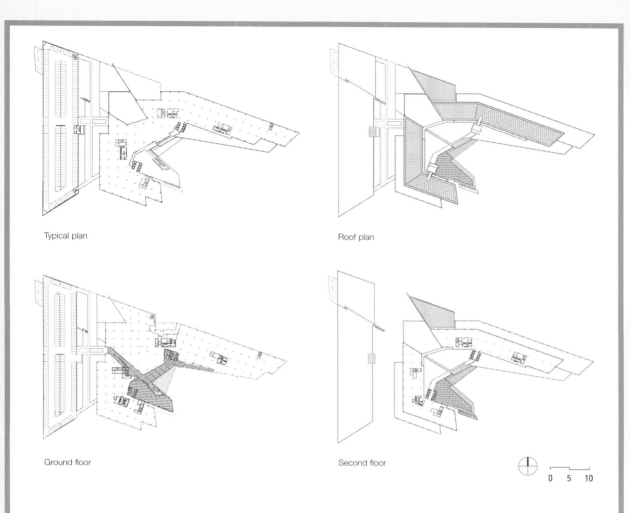

Typical plan

Roof plan

Ground floor

Second floor

0 5 10

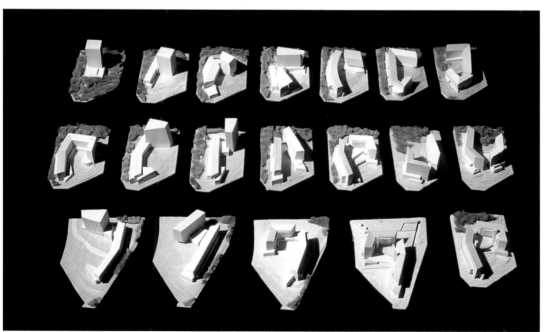

The transparency of the façades in the hallways, vestibules and other circulation areas emphasize the concept of community. The perception of internal movement brings the activities of the workers closer to the visitors and vice-versa.

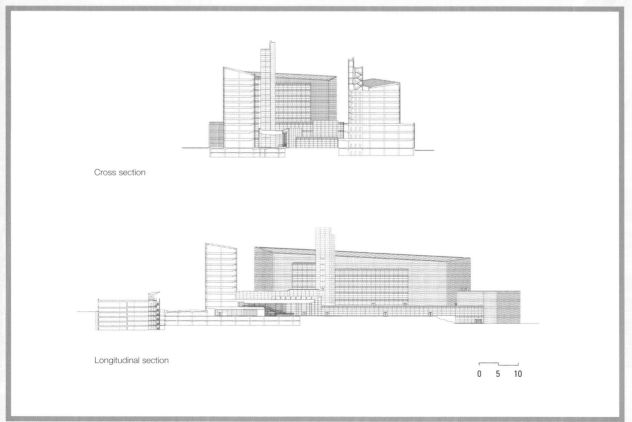

Cross section

Longitudinal section

0 5 10

The Institute is a place of research, teaching, and discussion: a forum for the exchange of ideas between visitors, academics, and students.

The scheme supports these aims by creating a building that is open and accessible, clear in its organization, and welcoming to its users. The proposal arranges the accommodation in a compact pavilion addressing the relandscaped Mansfield College gardens.

The library reading room is at the heart of the building design. It is a lofty, light-filled volume that overlooks the garden and serves both to identify the institute to the outside world and to provide a focus for the life within the building. In addition there are offices for visiting academics, seminar rooms, and a lecture hall.

The Institute is a modern interpretation of its neighbor, the Mansfield College library, a grade 1 listed neo-Gothic structure. Both buildings share a common organization, with the library set atop a plinth of teaching spaces; in both buildings, bay windows in the library become places for readers.

The plinth, sides, and back of the Institute are clad in the same bath stone as the older building. In contrast, on top, a delicate structure of glass and steel frames the library reading room and the triple height entrance hall. The fritted glass louvers provide solar and glare control, limiting the level of heat and light.

Oxford's brief requested a building without air conditioning, entirely cooled by natural ventilation. A clerestory with operable windows in the middle of the plan assures that this is successful. Night-time cooling and a thermal flywheel are controlled by a building maintenance system: all windows automatically open at night allowing the cool night air to be drawn into the building. The thermal mass provided by the exposed concrete frame and the books themselves allows the building to remain cool during the day.

Location: Oxford, England, UK
Date of construction: 2001
Client: Oxford University
Photographers: Peter Cook and H.G. Esch
Gross area: 26,800 sq. ft.

A strong ecological awareness guided the design of the building. It features a sophisticated natural ventilation system that does not require the installation of air conditioning.

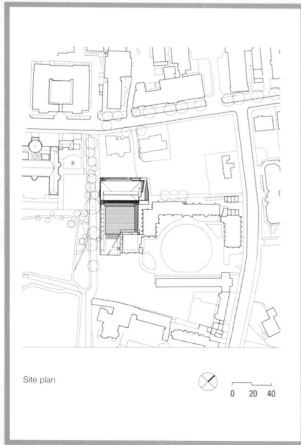

Site plan

0 20 40

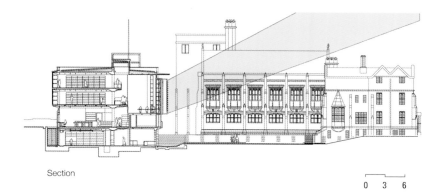

Section

0 3 6

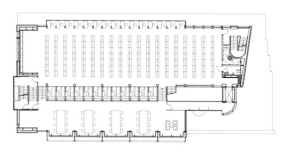

Second floor

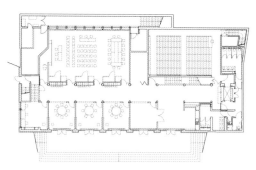

First floor

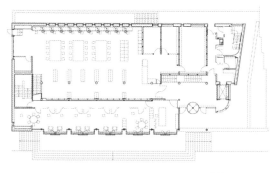

Ground floor

0 3 6

US Airways International Terminal One is part of a phased expansion of the Philadelphia Airport System, initiated in response to increased passenger traffic. The facility consists of a four-level terminal with 13 new international gates. Situated on the western edge of the runway, the building is linked to six existing terminals arranged to one side of a roadway.

The project brief mandated a design that satisfies the operational and spatial requirements of a modern terminal facility, but the siting posed a particular challenge. Hemmed to the north by the service road, the site area was originally conceived as a narrow rectangular band. This airside provision was ultimately insufficient, and to accommodate the demands of a complex program, Kohn Pedersen Fox proposed stretching the mass of Terminal One 190 feet over the roadway.

The novelty of this scheme is revealed in section. The approach to the terminal is defined by a large truss suspended 38 feet over the access road. All arrival functions—including baggage claim, a skylit arrivals hall, and the Federal Inspection Service (FIS)—are located on this level, one floor above the departure hall. This layout reverses the sectional sequence between arrival and departure, a transformation essential in the concept of the terminal as an international gateway. Distinct from traditional air transport facilities, which feature sunlit departure areas but afford deplaning passengers less than memorable amenities, arrival areas here are given equal architectural significance.

The quality of the space underneath the span is key to the design solution. The soffit acts as a weather-protected drop-off zone for departing travelers. Passengers enter the building through revolving doors along a clear glass curtain wall, and proceed to a double-height lobby with ticketing counters along the south wall. This concourse opens up to the arrivals level above, allowing daylight into the hall from the south and uniting the principal components of the program into an integrated composition of light, transparent spaces.

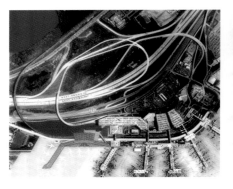

Location: Philadelphia, Pennsylvania, US
Client: US Airways
Date of construction: 1997–2002
Photographer: KPF
Rendering: AMD and dbox
Gross area: 750,000 sq. ft.

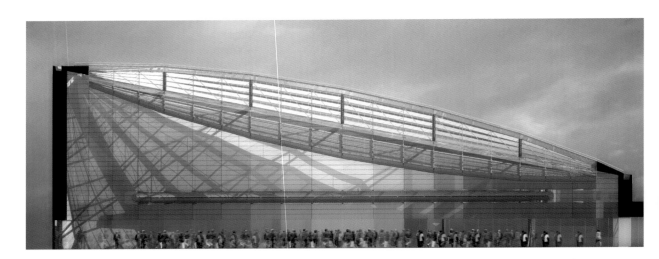

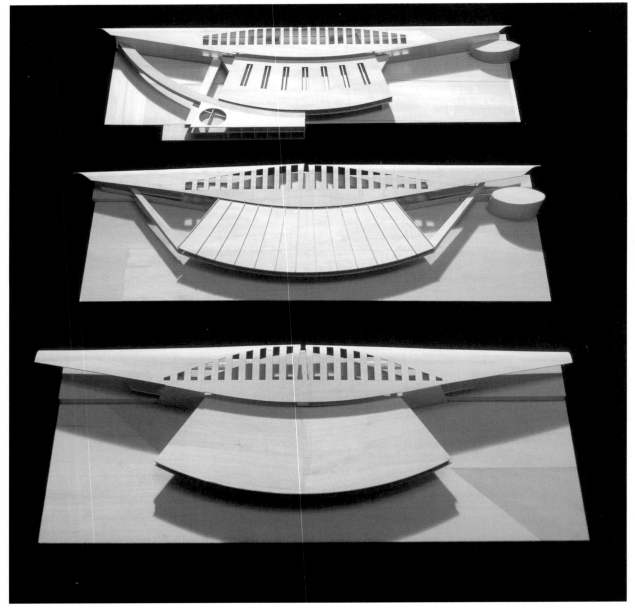

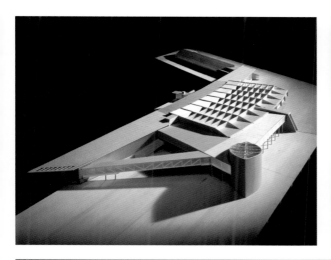

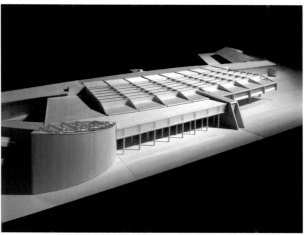

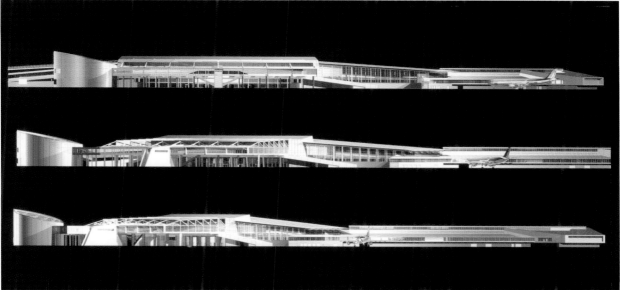

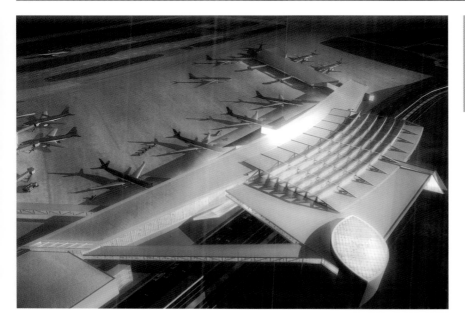

Models of different parts of the building and computer simulations afford reliable views of the future airport. By studying them fine-tuning can be done and modifications made to many aspects, prior to finalizing the project.

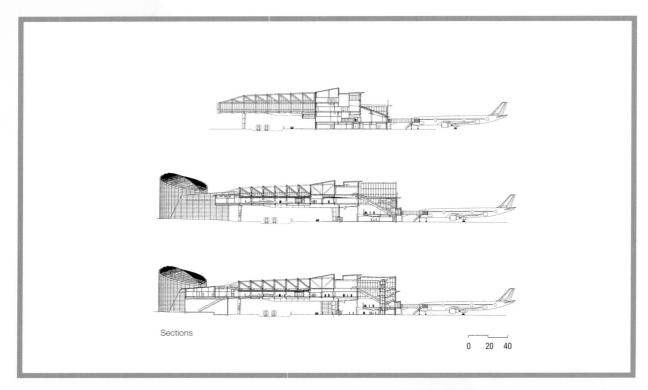

Sections

0   20   40

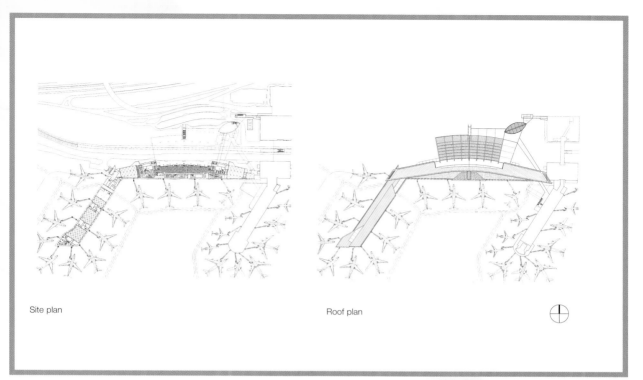

Site plan

Roof plan

The World Trade Center project is probably the most significant component in the emergence of Amsterdam's southern district as one of the leading business districts in Europe. Set apart from the old heart of the city, the area was initially developed to a master plan by H.P. Berlage which was somewhat compromised by post-1945 developments.

The existing World Trade Center consists of four multi-tenanted, mid-rise 1960s towers connected by lower structures and surrounded by open plazas, spaces which have been perceived as bleak and have consequently been little used. The intensification of uses in the surrounding area, where major road and rail routes are being covered with new office developments, provided an impetus to create attractive landscaped spaces with a much-needed conference center and shops and restaurants to serve the occupants of the World Trade Center and the wider public.

The key to the architects' proposals is the 323,000 sq. ft. freestanding, lightweight roof structure (designed in association with Guy Battle and RFR Paris) that wraps around the existing buildings to create a covered domain. The roof is far more than a cover: it incorporates opening vents and solar control panels to ensure comfortable conditions in the naturally ventilated spaces underneath. Fire control systems and acoustic panels are also incorporated into this innovative structure.

All the existing buildings are reclad as part of the scheme—the benefits of the overall roof as an environmental buffer extend to the strategy for naturally ventilating the office spaces and shading the facades. To the east, in a second phase of the project, a new 25-story tower will provide an extension to the Center, facing the existing buildings across a new public square on the line of Berlage's axis. The use of timber screens and colored panels, set behind the glazing, adds a rich texture to this new landmark structure. The entire project is, indeed, of wide significance as a demonstration of the way in which mono-cultural office districts can be transformed into mixed-use, round-the-clock city quarters.

Location: Amsterdam, The Netherlands
Date of construction: 1999–2002
Client: ING Vastgoed, Kantoren Fonds
Nederland Management
Photographers: Eammon O'Mahoney, E.G. Esch,
and Sjaak Henselmans
Gross area: 968,400 sq. ft.

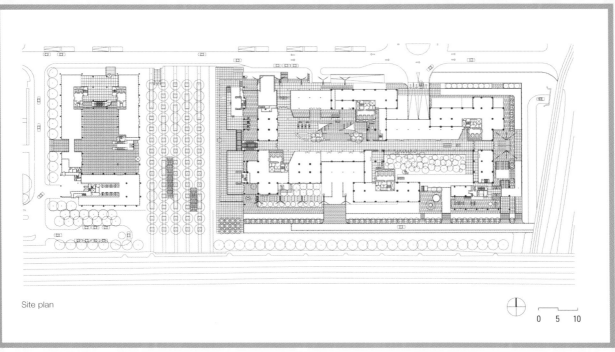

Site plan

0   5   10

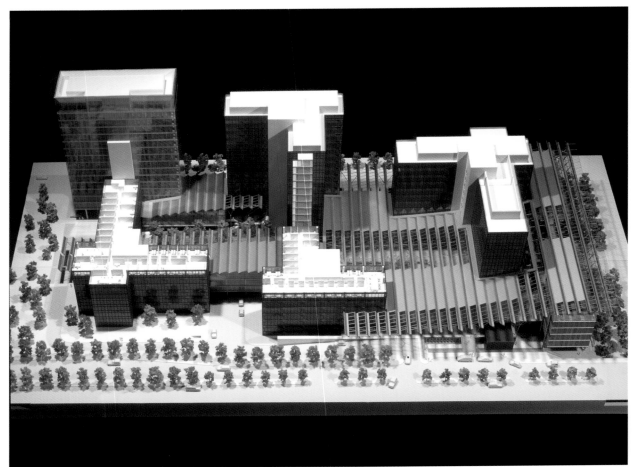

The building envelope, both the façade and the roof, is made up of a system of openings that reinforce the natural ventilation of the building, and thus minimize the need for air conditioning.

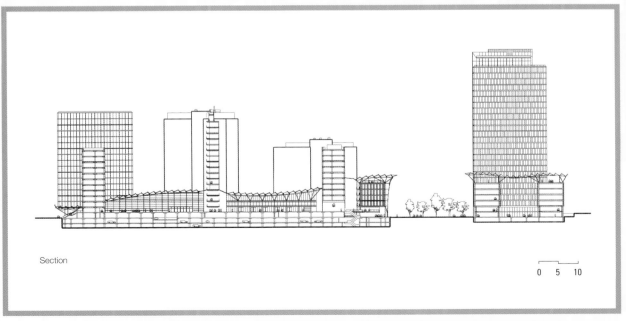

Section

0   5   10

The winning entry in an international competition, the Endesa project was seen by the client —a major national electricity utility— as an opportunity to mark its commitment to low-energy design and the development of a sustainable approach to building services. This agenda was addressed alongside a more strictly functional brief, that of bringing together a number of subsidiary companies previously scattered across a number of sites and creating a more efficient and interactive working environment. The site is on the edge of Madrid, in a new industrial and commercial quarter close to the M40 orbital motorway.

The scheme brings together operational and environmental objectives to memorable effect under a characteristic "big roof" which develops a theme seen in other low-rise office projects, including Thames Court in the city of London and the unbuilt KBB project in Dusseldorf. As at Thames Court, this 86,000 sq. ft. "fifth elevation" has a multi-functional character, acting as social space, environmental buffer and as an active "lung" to the building, expelling stale air and drawing in fresh. The extremes of the Madrid climate allow for the use of night cooling to counter the effect of very hot summer days. Louvers and shading devices ensure comfortable conditions in the atrium, while maintaining evenly daylit conditions. The atrium is seen as an essentially public and communal space, open to all. A clear symbol of the ecological thinking behind the scheme, it equally makes financial sense since the facades which it encloses are internal, so reducing construction costs. Photovoltaic units attached to the roof contribute significantly to the building's energy needs.

The offices are arranged as a series of 59-foot deep bars, with five levels of office accommodation above ground. Extensive parking areas are located on two basement levels. The design of external facades has been carefully tailored to meet the exigencies of the climate and baffle glare and solar gain. The whole project marries environmental concerns more typical of Northern Europe with the Mediterranean typology of the sheltered courtyard.

Location: Madrid, Spain
Date of construction: 1999–2002
Client: Grupo Endesa
Photographers: Eammon O'Mahoney and KPF
Gross area: 86,000 sq. ft.

For the project the typical Mediterranean typology of the building with patio, was chosen. For the headquarters of Endesa a glass covered roof made up of metal trusses and glass, covers a vast space six storeys high.

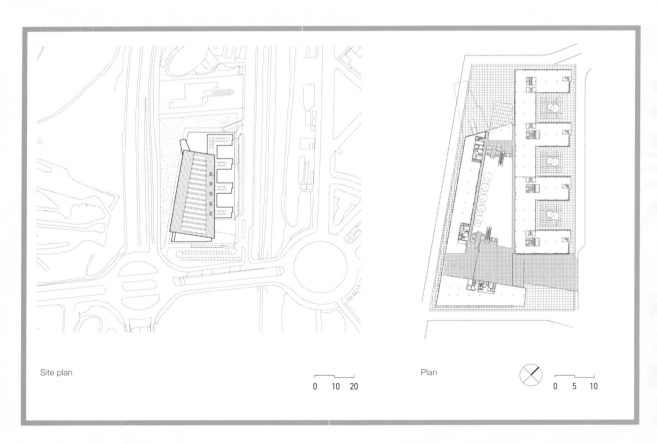

Site plan

0 10 20

Plan

0 5 10

Huge metal tubes that evacuate the air on the roof are used for the ventilation of the building, which makes use of both natural and forced ventilation.

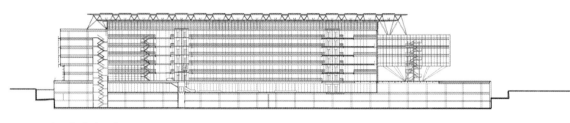

Longitudinal section

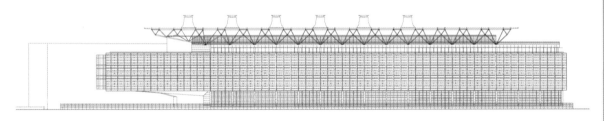

Elevation

0   4   8

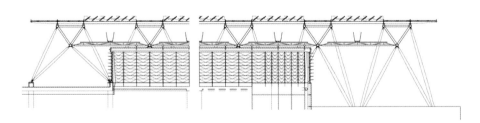

Detail

When it is completed, the Shanghai World Financial Center will stand as the tallest building in the world.

The project is located on a key site in the Lujiazhui financial and trade district in Pudong, which the Chinese government has designated as an Asian center for international banking and commercial interests. The rapid development of the zone has inevitably resulted in a disjunctive urban fabric to which the design of the tower reacts in its great monolithic simplicity.

The program of this 95-story project is contained within two distinctly formal elements: a sculpted tower and a podium. Corresponding to the Chinese concept of the earth as a square and the sky as a circle, the interaction between these two geometric forms gives shape to the tower. The project relates to its context through an abstract language that attempts symbolically to incorporate characteristics meaningful to the traditions of Chinese architecture, but is not limited to pictorial or image-based historical precedents.

The primary form of the tower is a square prism intersected by two sweeping arcs, tapering into a single line at the apex. The gradual progression of floor plans generates configurations that are ideal for offices on the lower floors and hotel suites above. At the same time, the transformation of the plan rotates the orientation of the upper portion of the tower toward the Oriental Pearl TV tower, the area's dominant landmark, a fifth of a mile away. To relieve wind pressure, a 164-foot (50-meter) cylinder is carved out of the top of the building. Equal in diameter to the sphere of the television tower, this void connects the two structures across the urban landscape. Wall, wing, and conical forms penetrate through the massive stone base of the tower. The varied geometries of these smaller elements lend human scale, and organize the complexities of pedestrian movement at the point of entry, complementing the elemental form of the tower.

Associate architect: Mori Building Architects and Engineers
Location: Shanghai, China
Date of construction: 1994–2005
Client: Mori Building Co.
Photographers: Cristophe and KPF
Gross area: 3,408,600 sq. ft.

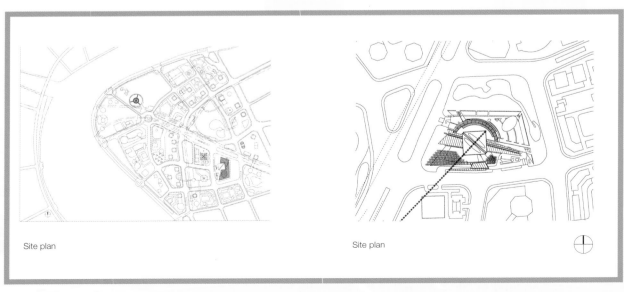

Site plan

Site plan

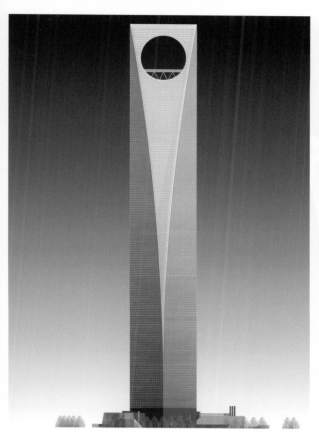

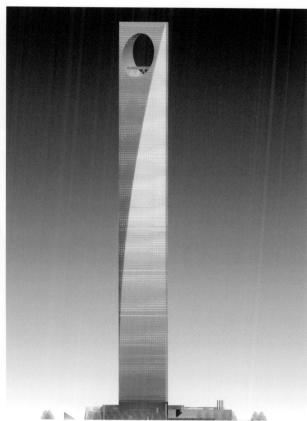

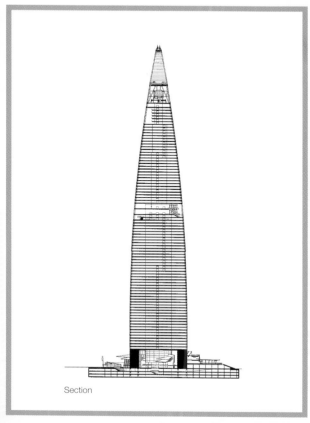

Section

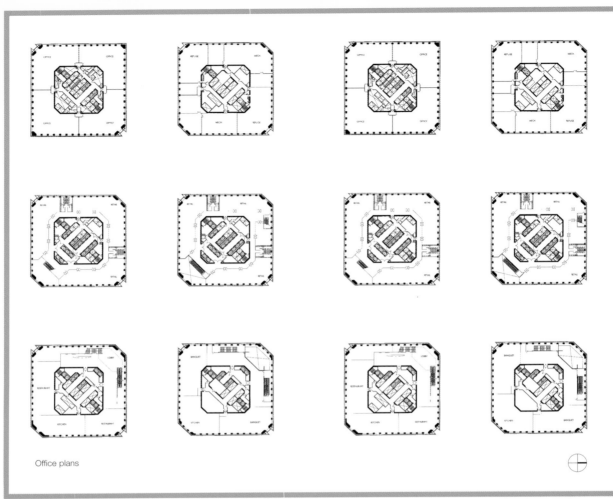

Office plans

The variation of forms on all of the floors of the building fashions a singular shape that varies according to the height. This type of distribution grants flexibility which favors a diversity of activities.

Hotel plans

This 108-story tower is the centerpiece of a master plan for a massive reclamation project in west Kowloon. Facing downtown Hong Kong across Victoria Harbor, the development was conceived as a transportation hub connecting Hong Kong to Chep Lap Kok airport, and a new urban center comprised of residential, office, retail, hotel, and recreation uses.

The brief for the Kowloon Station Tower included a 2.7 million sq. ft. office provision, together with a 300-room boutique hotel, and an observation deck on the 90th floor. Office floors are very generous in scale, with central cores. The hotel rooms occupy the upper levels of the tower, radiating from a cylindrical atrium topped by a restaurant. A vertical city all by itself, the tower will be one of the tallest structures in the world upon completion in 2008.

The winning entry in a design competition, the success of the scheme lies in the way in which the high-rise building form is welded into a highly efficient structural and operational agenda. Square in plan, the tower's reentrant corners taper to create a graceful profile against the sky. At its base, the tower splays out, creating an impression of a plant emerging from the ground. The walls of the tower peel away at the base, creating canopies on three sides, and a dramatic atrium on the north side. The atrium gestures towards the rest of the development and serves as a public linkage space to the retail and rail station functions. The concept of the building as a plant is further articulated as its crown assumes flower-like qualities of slenderness, transparency, and delicacy. The four façade elements extend up beyond the roof and slope back to create the building's profile. During the day, the transparent crown dissolves against the sky; at night this volume will appear as a glowing beacon.

The overall simplicity of the tower's form belies a richly textured cladding system, made up of glass and metal shingles, each a story high. These shingles serve to further dematerialize the tower, breaking up its mass as it reflects the sky, giving its form an appearance of great lightness.

Associate architect: Wong & Ouygang
Location: Hong Kong, China
Date of construction: 2000–2008
Client: Sun Hung Kai Properties
Photographers: Jock Pottle and KPF
Redering: AMD, Geopod, and dbox
Gross area: 3,200,000 sq. ft.

The glass-covered skin of the building seems to peel away from the structure and form the entrance to the tower. The façade becomes a porch that leads to a square with gardens that is laid out in front of the building.

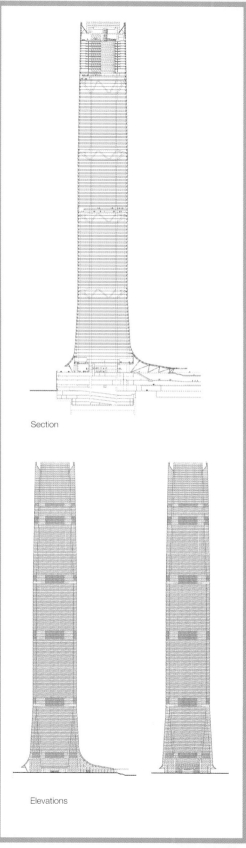

Section

Elevations

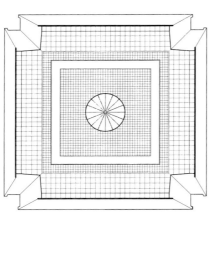

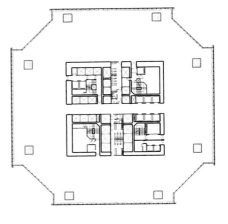

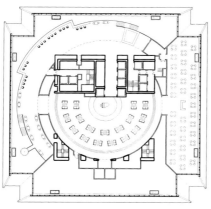

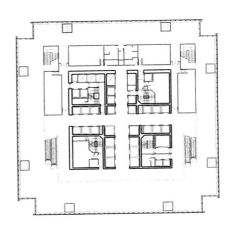

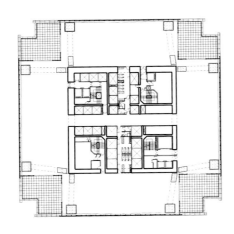

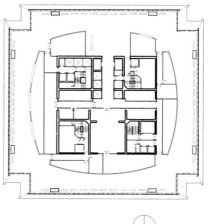

Plans

0   20   40

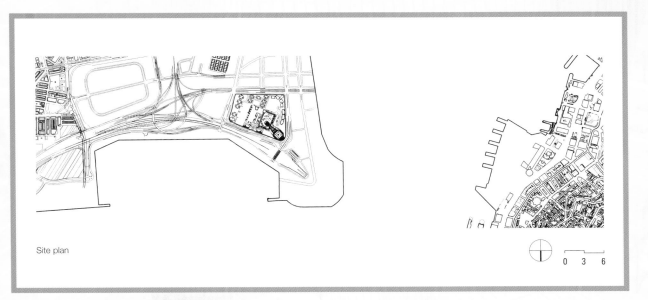

Site plan

0 3 6

New York Jets Stadium

The new home of the New York Jets football team is a 75,000-seat, open air stadium proposed for a site between 30ᵗʰ and 34ᵗʰ streets on Manhattan's west side. The focus of a redeveloped Hudson River waterfront, the stadium will be built on a deck above an existing rail yard, with an extensive public plaza and a multipurpose convention space on the 34ᵗʰ street side.

Aside from holding the ten National Football League games played per season, the stadium will also incorporate expanded convention facilities for the adjacent Jacob Javits Center. As New York City looks toward the possibility of hosting the 2012 Olympiad, the stadium is designed to expand to meet the requirements of the International Olympic Committee.

A principal consideration of the design is the integration of the development into the immediate context. On axis with the Empire State Building, the stadium continues the city grid, and with the addition of the public park, unites the neighborhoods of north Chelsea and Hell's Kitchen with the river. In plan and elevation, the scheme suggests an "inland pier," formally establishing a relationship with the artifacts of the city's maritime history. The design also preserves and extends the Highline, an elevated two-track freight train platform running 1.6 miles from Gansevoort Street in Greenwich Village to 34ᵗʰ street and Eleventh Avenue. Built in the 1930s as part of the West Side Improvement, the now-derelict platform is reconceived as an historic opportunity to create an elevated green space connected to the stadium's landscape program.

The scheme is a significant departure from conventional sports facilities-planning in North America. It promotes an unprecedented, environmentally sensitive agenda for a building of this type. Through the use of over 100,000 sq. ft. of solar panels, 36 wind turbines, rainwater collection, and wastewater treatment, the stadium complex is conceived as entirely self-sustaining—able to generate energy for itself and the surrounding city grid.

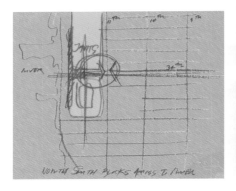

Location: New York, New York, US
Client: New York Jets
Photographers: Jock Pottle and KPF
Gross area: 2,600,000 sq. ft.

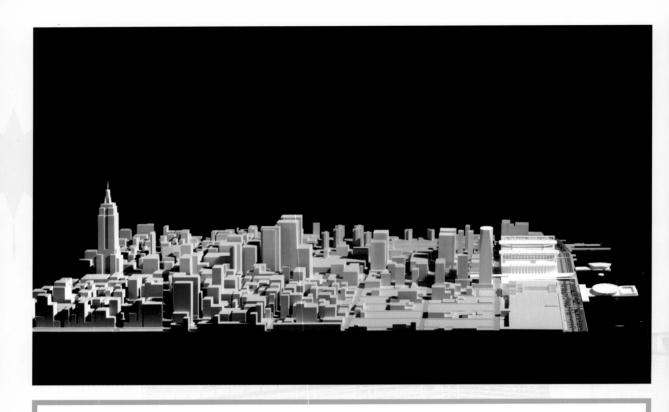

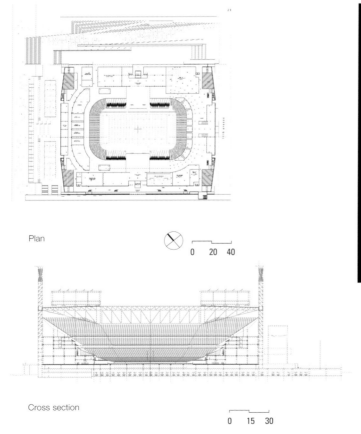

Plan

0   20   40

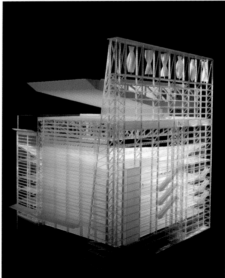

The installation of solar panels on most of the façade of the stadium makes this the first energy self-sufficient sports installation.

Cross section

0   15   30

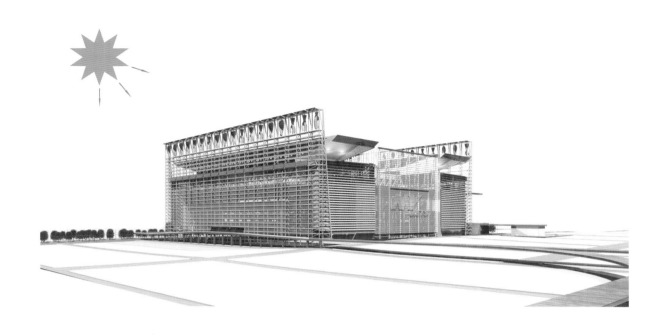

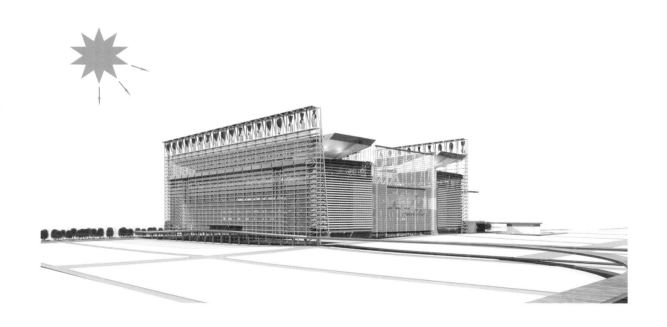

In 2002, *New York Magazine* invited KPF to submit an innovative design for the World Trade Center (WTC) site. Our scheme creates a sky memorial passage rising out of the water at the southern tip of Manhattan, at the departure point of the ferries to the Statue of Liberty. It rises at a slope of $1/12$ (to accommodate the disabled) above West Street and spirals around the site of the WTC, culminating in an iconic tower 2001 feet in height. The city streets which surround the site either pass through (Greenwich Street) or have visual access across the site. The development parcels resulting from this gesture are scaled to work with the proper dimensions for office, in the main body of the site, or residential, along West Street. This scheme can accommodate 7 million square feet on the original site, along with an additional 3 million square feet along West Street.

We envision it as a unifying conceptual element which can be formed over buildings below—in a sense creating a zoning envelope which can be economically achieved as an integrated part of the construction of individual buildings. Specifically, the memorial skyway is not constructed as a structure in itself, except for bridging from building to building.

We propose to build structures on top of the lowered West Street, and then place our sky promenade upon these structures. Great portals, framed between the buildings, invite one from outside to inside. These portals dominate the unique identity of separate real estate entities, yet each building's function is uncompromised. The east side of Manhattan is then stitched to the west side along this seam, which becomes a higher version of Manhattan's existing "high line."

A spiraled enclosure defines an urban space both inside and outside its walls, and a substantial variety of urban rooms result. One of the more interesting is the east–west wedge-shaped space, which is terminated by St. Paul's Chapel. The dominant civic room, which is formed by the spiral, can contain the exact memorial footprints of the two towers, as pools of water. Greenwhich Street passes through this room. In addition, this space is activated by the public ascending to the top of the 2001-foot tower. Lifts to the memorial skyway are also included adjacent to the tower.

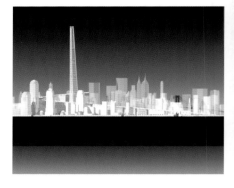

Location: Lower Manhattan, New York, US
Client: Lower Manhattan Development
Corporation
Date of project: 2002

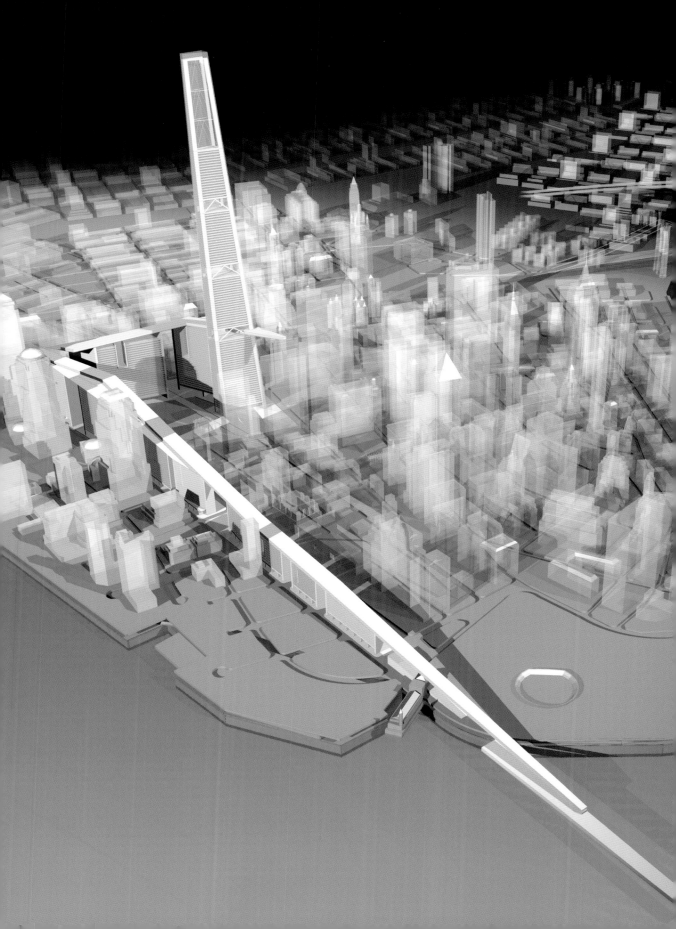

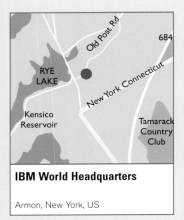

IBM World Headquarters

Armon, New York, US

Provinciehuis

The Hague, The Netherlands

Baruch College Academic Complex

New York City, New York, US

Gannett/USA TODAY Corporate Headquarters

McLean, Virginia, US

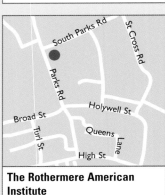

The Rothermere American Institute

Oxford, England

Philadelphia International Airport

Philadelphia, Pennsylvania, US

World Trade Center Amsterdam

Amsterdam, The Netherlands

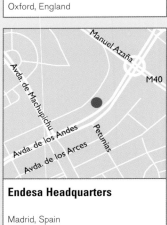

Endesa Headquarters

Madrid, Spain

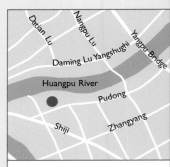

Shanghai World Financial Center

Shanghai, China

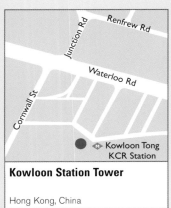

Kowloon Station Tower

Hong Kong, China

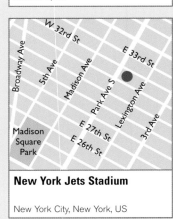

New York Jets Stadium

New York City, New York, US

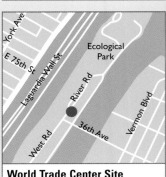

World Trade Center Site Development

Manhattan, New York, US

Chronology of Works

1980   AT&T Long Lines Eastern Regional Headquarters, Oakton, Virginia , US

1983   333 Wacker Drive, Chicago, Illinois, US

1985   Procter & Gamble World Headquarters, Cincinnati, Ohio, US

1992   1250 Boulevard René-Lévesque, Montréal, Québec, Canada

1992   Goldman Sachs European Headquarters, London, UK

1993   Westendstraße 1, DG Bank Headquarters, Frankfurt, Germany

1995   First Hawaiian Center, Honolulu, Hawai, US

1996   World Bank Headquarters, Washington DC, US

1997   Buffalo Niagara International Airport, Buffalo, New York, US

1997   Mark O. Hatfield United States Courthouse, Portland, Oregón, US

1997   IBM World Headquarter, Armonk, New York, US

1998   Samsung Plaza Rodin Pavilion, Seoul, South Korea

1998   Thames Court, London, UK

2000   One Raffles Link, Singapore

2001   New Academic Complex, Baruch College, New York, New York, US

2001   Gannett/USA Today Corporate Headquarters, McLean, Virginia, US

2001   Rothermere American Institute, Oxford University, Oxford, UK

2002   World Trade Center Extension, Amsterdam, The Netherlands

2002   745 Seventh Avenue, New York, New York, US